SCHOLASTIC

Let's Find Out™

Let's Play a Five Senses Guessing Game

Amanda Miller · Joan Michael

Children's Press®
A Division of Scholastic Inc.
New York Toronto London Auckland Sydney
Mexico City New Delhi Hong Kong
Danbury, Connecticut

Literacy Specialist: Francie Alexander, Chief Academic Officer, Scholastic Inc.
Art Director: Joan Michael

Photographs: James Levin (gold coins, dirty socks, colored duct tape, all photos of boy); ©William A. Bolton/Alamy (fall foliage detail); ©Bob Elsdale/Getty Images (rabbit); ©Canopy Photography/Veer (mouse); ©Darrin Klimek/Getty Images (towels); ©Digital Vision/Getty (Sharpei); ©Fancy Photography/Veer (fall foliage); ©Food Collection/Getty Images (lemons); ©GK Hart/Vikki Hart/Getty Images (frog); ©Iconica/Getty Images (pie); ©Image Source (perfume bottle); ©Photodisc (watermelon, pepper, pinecone); ©Photodisc/Veer (macaw, jingle bells, pretzel); ©Photonica/Getty (crying baby); ©Stockdisc/Getty Images (tiara)

Library of Congress Cataloging-in-Publication Data

Miller, Amanda, 1974-
   Let's play a five senses guessing game / written by Amanda Miller.
      p. cm. — (Let's find out)
   ISBN-13: 978-0-531-14871-6 (lib. bdg.)
   ISBN-10: 0-531-14871-8 (lib. bdg.)
   1. Senses and sensation—Juvenile literature. I. Title. II. Series.

QP434.M54 2007
612.8—dc22   2006026329

1 2 3 4 5 6 7 8 9 10 R 16 15 14 13 12 11 10 09 08 07

I use my five senses every day. So do you!
Let's play a five senses guessing game.

I **see** with my eyes.
I look at the world around me.
There's so much to see every day.

Here is what I saw today.

shiny coins

a sparkly tiara

a colorful bird

a wrinkled dog

Look at my shiny treasure!

what did you
See today?
How did it
look?

I hear with my ears.
I listen carefully to hear soft sounds.
I cover my ears when sounds are too loud!

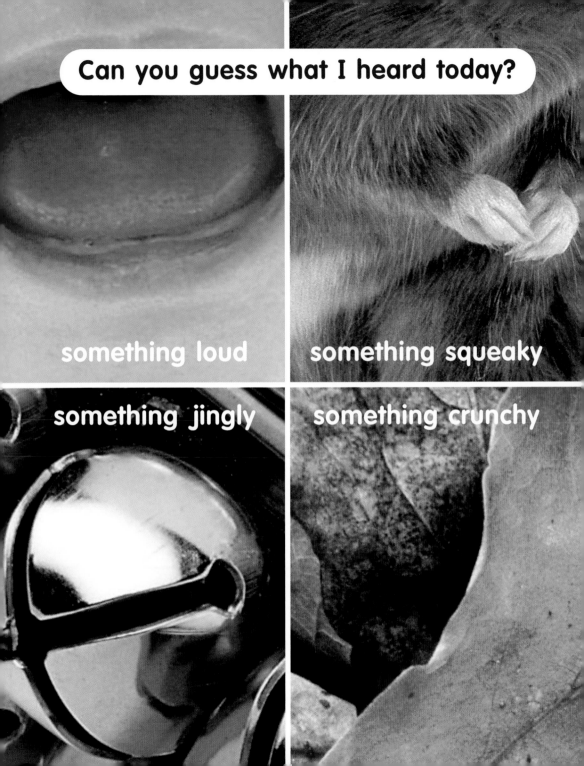

Here is what I heard today.

a loud baby

a squeaky mouse

crunchy leaves

jingly bells

Stop that loud crying!!!!!

what did you **hear** today?
How did it **Sound**?

I smell with my nose.
Sniff, sniff! Some things smell good
and some things don't!

Here is what I smelled today.

a stinky sock

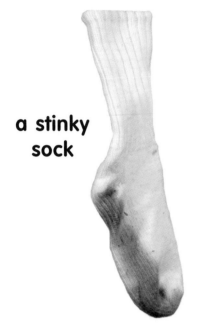

flowery perfume

fresh towels

a sweet pie

EEWWW! Stinky!

what did you **Smell** today?
How did it **Smell**?

I taste with my tongue.
I like to try
new foods.
There are lots
of wonderful
things to taste!

Here is what I tasted today.

a sweet watermelon

a sour lemon

a spicy pepper

a salty pretzel

what did you **taste** today? How did it **taste**?

Yum! So Sweet!

I touch things with my fingers to learn how they feel. I also feel with my skin. A cool breeze feels good on my face and arms.

Can you guess what I touched today?

something sticky

something slippery

something prickly

something soft

Here is what I touched today.

sticky tape

a slippery frog

a soft bunny

a prickly pinecone

yikes!
So Sticky!

what did you **touch** today?
How did it **feel**?

Sometimes, I use all my senses together. That's why I love popcorn!

How does it look? Fluffy!

How does it sound? Crunchy!

How does it smell? Buttery!

How does it taste? Salty!

How does it feel? Bumpy!

How did you use all your senses today?